I0407328

THE PERSONAL REVOLUTION OF FACUNDO MARVAL

A novel

Luis Carlos Márquez

Copyright © 2012 de Luis Carlos Márquez

ISBN-13: 978-1540837684

ISBN-10: 1540837688

To Jacqueline, my wife, who gave me the companionship, support and understanding that made my life possible and my later years very happy, thanks to my best and only friend.

Also to my two girls, Carla and Beatriz, because without them my life would not be complete.

~

Many stories never get written, because despite of being true, are utterly unbelievable. Reality outdoes fiction all the time.

~

CONTENTS

Foreword
Part I - The Golden Trail
Part II - The Duchess
Part III - Mount Pleasant
Acknowledgments

FOREWORD

One of the most difficult things in life is to foresee what effect will, an event have in our lives. Will it enhance our lives or not? Will it bring good or bad luck? If I hadn't taken the mad decisions that I have in my life, in addition to being at a specific time and place, I probably would not be here today. Not that I wanted to make mad decisions, I just did. It came natural to me. As a consequence of those very mad decisions I am now living one of the best periods of my life. No doubt the outcome was totally unexpected and contradictory. How did that happen? Is there such a thing as an orderly chaos?

I am convinced everything happens for a reason and every event (good or bad) leads us to unforeseeable different directions. The sequence is vital and crucial to the final outcome, so is luck, which is so unpredictable that even being a direct consequence of that sequence, it could very well end up as the opposite of what we expect.

The Personal Revolution of Facundo Marval takes a glimpse at this fascinating and mysterious aspect of life, by following his personal golden trail and his personal revolution. Five people end up being persecuted and eventually separated, by the ideals of a revolution that did not exist.

This book is a work of fiction. Names characters, places and incidents are the product of the author's imagination or are used fictionally, and any resemblance to actual persons, living or dead, events, or locations is entirely coincidentally.

I The Golden Trail

Life is slipping by
Ignoring me
I must write, on and on…

Leaving words
Along the golden trail
As autumn leaves
One by one

As autumn leaves
One by one
To keep you warm from chilly winds
And give your soul a sunny glow

To leave a sign
For you to follow
And find me far away over the hill

Hopefully before sunset
Hopefully, hopefully…
Before, I am long gone.

Chapter 1

Everyone has a golden trail laid out for them. We tend to think that it starts when we are born, but sometimes it's a continuation of our ancestor's. No matter what we do or don't, we will inevitably end up within it, because it's our one and only life.

At a point in his life Facundo Marval, my father, wrote these prophetic words, which opened the written statement of a visionary dream that spearheaded to a place way far in the future…

"And life went through me like a ray of light leaving very little behind and I was totally replaced. Only two generations had passed and I have been already forgotten, as well as millions before me. I am sad because my life has come and gone so soon, but glad because I have lived it and know life will continue for many others after me. It is our destiny…The grandson of my grandson, who had since then also disappeared, was reading a virtual digest magazine. I was long gone. He doesn't have a family name anymore because it had since been replaced by a number. The article he is reading is projected into a kind of suspended "ether", which is a reflection of his mind visualized right in front of his eyes, which are not used for their conventional purpose anymore, like a dream. No one else can see the vision, because it is projected in tune with his own unique frequency and key. While he is concentrated in his "lecture" he is virtually transposed to his next destination monitored by a trillion sensors which control his route and actions. The vision makes reference to the time when still there were countries, because this concept did not exist anymore. It was since abolished because it became the main source of misunderstanding, selfishness and differences. Reality had gone virtual, silently becoming data, just numbers. Transportation as we know it disappeared. It was easier to bring places and events to us wireless or transpose us. Of course this was done by his avatar; he himself was enclosed in a command module capsule with a cycle span of five hundred years renewable, and everything is going so fast that

he is learning a new life each day. By then people died like old lions when failing to maintain their virtual territory, alone and estranged, disconnected and instantly pulverized. Cemeteries disappeared long ago, realizing that after two generations tombs and mausoleums became deserted. An exception was granted for those who had become famous or valuable to humanity and their pulverized ashes were kept in special places "cocoons" were these valuable legacies were kept. Only the pulverized ashes of intellectuals who evoked rational thinking where deposited in these places of distinction for the collective memory to revere. Everyone else passed anonymously. In between time many organizational changes had taken place. Individual enterprises ceased to exist and replaced by specialized sectors, the principle of competition replaced by cooperation and optimization. The leaders of such sectors made choices within their jurisdictions and ultimately attended a representative global network of all sectors for the purpose of final decision making. The main criterion was that every decision had to be unanimously taken to ensure the benefit of all. Heads of state, revolutionaries, dictators, kings and such, who acted in the name of the people, together with their respective systems of government became a thing of the past. Cancer and terrorism were eradicated and almost forgotten they had ever existed. This was the world were the grandson of my grandson, who had since then also disappeared, existed..."

This was my father's interpretation of what would come out of the personal revolution he started within himself in 1941, the year I was born. Provided every living person concurrently underwent their own personal revolution, and individually and collectible changed the way we now think. Often he will remind himself and us "My writing will save me, my writing will save us all"

Now, at seventy five, I am here in my old age, perplexed, looking a little to the past, trying to focus on the present and avoiding to peek much at the future because I see the end rushing to snatch my body, or my soul, or both...

However convinced, that idealist men, like my father, are the ones that lay the prints to the unthinkable. Now I am doing my bit of the same and will continue to do so as long as I am able.

If there was a next life and I could live again I would like to be an astrophysicist, so I could dream realities in a grand scale and look mostly outwards, to ignore the sordidness that goes about me now. The first thing I would discover is that life does not belong to anyone, it belongs to all. This would become the core of my philosophy and the sieve through which I would separate what is essential than what is not.

You see, once you have the privilege to look out at the universe and understand what goes on out there, one has no choice than to conclude that we are also integral part of all those wonders. Once that is understood, the logical thing is to look inwards and try to figure out the meaning of what we have been so fortunate to discover.

After panning my surrounding for a while I concluded that greed is the root of all age's problems. Obviously the solution should be more distribution of richness, but egoism doesn't allow it. A valid question: I earned it, why should I give it away? A valid answer: For the survival of the human race, in other words your own survival. Easy to understand: Yes. Easy to do: Not really…

***

Facundo Marval, my father, was a true revolutionary, a positive one: not a communist, not a socialist, not an anti-imperialist, not an anti-capitalist. He was simply an individualist, who believed in a "live and let live" approach to change.

The kind that grows from time to time in Latin America around the Caribbean, floating between the swaying palm trees and the ferns of the gigantic mountains that guard the north coast of *Little Venice* from invaders. The kind that always pays a price for what they are. In these parts revolutionaries are as common as green tropical lizards, they are everywhere.

Baby Facundo was lulled to sleep every day, by the caress of his mother chanting a traditional lullaby.

"Duérmase mi niño,
Que tengo que hacer,
Lavar los pañales y hacer de comer..."

This became the inner sound of his soul. The sweet vibrations that commanded him to be a good leader of his own destiny, responsible only to himself, because in these parts leaders do not follow the rules, they make them. Very early on, he became notorious for getting into trouble at school because of that very fact. His teachers complained that he did not comply with anything. He was chronically late, seldom had his homework completed, his gaze was lost somewhere in time and quarreled easily with other classmates for anything at all. He became a major headache for the school principal and subject of his own study.

Oddly enough at home he was a quite gentle boy, helping in everything and obeying faithfully his mother's requests, to the point that he appeared to be another person altogether. His mother could not understand what the fuzz of the school was about and was convinced that was not her Facundo's behavior, but indeed it was, two personalities embodying one.

He was not influenced by his father because his father was never around, because he was busy getting into his own kind of troubles. Instead my father inherited most of his mother's character: strong, independent and courageous. The qualities that make single mothers survive and controversial dreams alive.

Facundo's dreams were nursed by the purity of the oxygen of the Caribbean breeze, the music of the swaging coconut palms and the majestic tranquility of the shade of the tropical mangos, which spread all along the coast and covered the valley like a green velvet gigantic quilt. His goals were so pure and simple that they became impossible to understand

By the time he was thirteen, he was already on the subversive list of the dictatorial regime of the time. When he reached eighteen, prompted by the early death of his father, leaving his mother behind for the time being, he decided to make his own world in a way different than anything known until then, simple and plain.

He ran far away, cleared a patch of land somewhere between the Orinoco and the Amazon River, far enough from any civilized entity so he could be his own master, construct and live his own life. Which latter proved to be almost impossible due to the conditions prevailing at the time. Nevertheless he went and by instinct seemed to already know the ways of the jungle as if he lived there in a previous life.

In time he came across a small tribe that eventually took him in as one of his own. Following the tradition, by competition, he won the privilege to become the life companion of the eldest daughter of the chief. In time they had a son (me) and name him Facundo as well.

***

Where I am now I turn to the past to rescue a little of my own self, which I have inadvertently left behind for so many years and it may come handy for the events that are still to come. I have a little time left and I am still able to recall…

My first tools were the ones which came with my Ma's Singer sewing machine, in a small chromed tool box. With those I constructed my first make believe cars and planes and motorcycles. I was nine years old, it was 1950. What a divine age to be, my voice hadn't changed yet but I wasn't a kid either…

Since the beginning Ma tried to enhance my heritage by telling me stories about the starting years with Pa. She described him as a practical man and her as possessing the otherwise unobtainable common sense one inherits from generations living in the wild.

She recalls that when it came time to select the site for what now is the main building in our ranch, she suggested waiting, until the rains were in full force to select the highest ground.

The building was started and finish during the dry season. She insisted the house to be whitewashed. When Pa asked why, she simply answered: Because the sky is blue and the grass is green and roses are red...houses are white. This extremely detailed sense of naturalistic relationships made everything she touched, perfect.

It was possible for her to illustrate these tangible concepts, because we actually were surrounded by such beauty: endless blue skies, green rolling hills, and a million shades of red, nature's perfect background and of course our bright white washed house in the middle, shaded by gorgeous mango trees, spreading like majestic guards on both sides of the brown serpent country road that led to our courtyard.

When it came time to select the working horses, Ma insisted in the sorrel color. She believed that was the original color horses came to be and when it came time to choose the color of the guard dogs she could not thing of another than black, because she said they became invisible at night and that was the way it was supposed to be.

***

Around that time my grandma (from Pa's side) came to live with us in the town of El Dorado, while my mother alternated between the house and my father's cattle ranch. Ma would stay two weeks at a time at the ranch's rural cottage, cooking, cleaning, ironing and taking care of the orchard, the flower patch and generally providing a home for father. And father would come home with her, two weeks at a time, to our home at El Dorado to pick supplies, seeds, vaccines, spare parts, burb wire, nails, tools and any other thing needed for the up keeping of the cattle ranch.

At that time the valuable lecture learned was humility and patience, because things were slow. We learned that nothing worthwhile happens instantly, not even birth or death, both require a lot of effort and humility and patience. Humility and patience makes life more livable under any circumstance.

The screws and bolts were not easy to handle and frustration - the main enemy - was always stalking me. As a child I realized that one conquers failure by repetition, one learns by doing again and again the same thing in different ways, and due time one of the ways would work. Eventually frustration goes away as one learns and masters the art. Getting familiar with failure became then a liberating feeling.

At that time everything was looked at, through a white thin lace veil, with the intention of protecting oneself from being overwhelmed. But also this requirement made everything very difficult to understand. Things were not clear at all.

I didn't realize it then, but I lived in a paper world. Paper file cabinets where in every room of the house. I didn't care much either, since everything went on without my concurrence and my real world went on in my head anyway, and it had nothing to do with reality.

Often I did hear my Pa said that "Paper can stand anything". That didn't make sense to me at all, because I thought paper was fragile and thin. What good was it to me anyway - since most of my own things went on in my head - but if I had to choose a material, pig iron or led would have done fine, or any other materials could have done just as well, even wood. Plastic was not so much around those days, but certainly I wouldn't have chosen paper.

Much, much latter, I found out that really everything had to do with paper: money, stocks, bonds, contracts, birth certificates, marriage certificates, death certificates…not to mention decrees, laws and even the constitution. Everything!

***

My second tool was my Ma's diary, which she let me read from time to time as I grew older, to provide me with inside as to whom I was and where did I come from, and why my father was not anymore with us…

The diary was written in an almost allegoric poetic style, which was very pleasant to hear and to read, but a tat difficult to understand. One had to read it over and over again and at times even read between the lines to catch the meaning of what was said, as if it was written in an ancient code.

Something, like this:

"He moved silently, inconspicuously, aloof like death itself. His gaze was partially ferocious and partially naive. He only killed for the right to survive and yet he was feared by all. On a patch of green forest land 20 kilometers west of El Dorado and 15 kilometers south to the Amazon River, lingers the scent of The Jaguar. Elusive, dark, soundless, strides between sunsets and sundown`s when he sets himself into a hunting motion and begins to pace the grey, black and occasional tints of green which mark the silhouette of this part of the world, during the dim hours, when everything seems to stand still but it is not. When you come from as far away as he comes you arrive tired. If he was asked, and could answer, he would only say that he suffered and would suffer more about what he says. All the stories of survival are like that. It would not be possible to make him do or say anything he didn't want to, because he had no debts to be paid and nothing to acquire. He owned and had everything he needed. He was not a soldier, or merchant, or religious, or scientific being. His name was Maru and he was only an animal. But if he had a choice he would like to be a philosopher, the purest of meaning and in that case just live in peace and write what he thought and believe, preferable in a foreign language so he could not be censored and yet easily translated profusely. His writing would be simple, direct and honest. He would only practice the most disinterested of the arts, doing no harm, and his stories could be proven true by life itself. But none of that was possible because he was only an animal…"

The stories came with the diary and the land came with the animals and the people. In time the land was wasted and many of the people had disappeared, now the animals thrived and the stories staid along because it took only two to remember, my grandma and me. So

I set out to do what she would have done, remember and pass it on, write it on…

***

Eventually, rescuing my thoughts I pinned the fact that billions of years before any man sat foot on these lands everything was pure and simple, like only nature can be: colorful, fluid, clean, harmless, seasonal and astoundingly beautiful. Shapes and forms changed with the ages, and unhurriedly became what today we could envision as a paradise in one simple word. Then nothing changed for a long time.

***

In 1941, the year I was born, according to the story, my father introduced the Asian water buffalo to these lands, over seventy five years ago. In an effort to contribute a perfect match, thinking that the animal would adapt perfectly to the two seasons that we have there: six month of dry and six months of rain, similar to the ones in lands near the Asian equator. These animals have evolved to withstand the rigors of these extreme conditions for thousands of years: dry, dusty, extreme equatorial heat for six months and humid, flooded by the rain monsoons the rest of the year.

Pa brought two bulls and four pregnant cows all the way from India, across the Orinoco's river delta and then rafted them upstream and then herded them along until they reached the boundaries of his land. Two brand irons with the profile of The Jaguar's head where waiting the small herd for branding. The bulls burned first, then the four cows, and the calves when they reached three months.

Eventually the native people, which took a peak from time to time, began to call them the black cows with the backward horns,

"Las vacas negras con los cachos torcidos hacia atrás".

Very soon they became, as they grew in size and numbers, part of the landscape and made it more interesting still. The jaguars where curious, but respected them and did not dare to consider them prey yet. The small calves blended as if they were natural to these parts and my father, the buffaloes and the jaguars became an "understanding".

***

I was born rich in principles, but without any guaranties. There was no stability of any kind, in my family and in Little Venice. It was like living in a boat that was constantly about to sink. Water licking in everywhere and regardless of how much forward rowing one did, the boat seemed to stay put in the same place, it did not move. It appeared that most of the time was spent bailing. Generations became old, hopelessly bailing to keep the country afloat to no avail.

Silence is the most eloquent of expressions. At times it could mean total agreement or disagreement, declare or absolve guilt, highlight or dissipate doubts. Likewise it could cause irreparable harm when misunderstood.

For years I kept silence about these injustices, driven by my natural disposition to cause no harm, thinking that it was the best way to handle unfair treatment, because eventually good faith would prevail. Ignore it, I said to myself. But no, good faith was not recognised, until it was too late to do anything, except speak.

And so I did.

In the very start, the general was very popular with the poor, even though he was not a politician by career he managed to construct an agenda which promised to give poor people the necessities of life. Simultaneously he blamed the rich for all the hardships that the poor had to go through for hundreds of years and the hopeless state they found themselves. Additionally he went through a struck of luck when the price of black gold skyrocketed, which allowed him to give away free housing, free education and better paid jobs, all from the colossal stream of oil cash.

Unfortunately at the same time declared an informal war on the wealthy, forcing them to reduce investment and production or eventually close down. This produced a division in the population which persists until today.

The general infiltrated and politicized all the reminder powers: legislative, judiciary, and militarized and politicized service.

So at that time, Little Venice was governed by a host of villains who distributed the country among themselves, as if it was their private estate, establishing a tyranny. Like landlords, with all the prerogatives of a royal.

In reality they were primitive, simple minded, but with the power of a king, without any special abilities or common sense, settling matters (always in their favor) and running a reign of terror with iron fists. All this was allowed only because of spread ignorance and the mild nature of many people like my father, who were content to relinquish a huge portion of their liberties to have a so called "system of government", any system, which always did more harm than good.

People talked about a civil war, but it was just talk, because the dictator had a hold on the army and spend a lot of money on weapons and other systems of repression. Father always said that the writen and spoken word used wisely - in a pacific way - had the same effect of a ten megaton bomb. But the right to express ideas was also suppressed. So there was no other way than to go underground. Father started writing a weekly anonymous pamphlet called "The voice" and signed with the pseudonymous a common mind and finished his articles with the phrase "The mind is everything"

I am still heartbroken by the images of people queuing up to buy food, vehicles and machinery out of service for lack of spare parts, sickness spearheading for lack of medicines, dramatic crime explosion, inhuman political persecution, lack of justice and general corruption. There had been bad dictatorship before in *"Little Venice"*, but I am told this one - under The General - has been the worst in history. The other two did not apologise about being dictators, like a stern father, but they did something. Everything that is worthwhile today in Little Venice was built or started by them, and there was order. Because of them the term "Benevolent dictator" was inspired and coined.

What saddens me most now, is to see ones country being destroyed by a bunch of hoodlums and the feeling of frustration one sees in the face of millions of people, because very little can be done, at least for the time being. Many things were wrong at that time, but the worst was a complete disregard for the constitution and neglect of the elder and children, the most vulnerable. And the poor stray skinny street dogs, which had consumed themselves to the bare bone like skeletons that refuse to die, scavenging around the garbage cans, like a loud complain from the higher forces of nature to such barbaric behavior…

Whenever I allowed myself to think about the poor stray skinny street dogs of Little Venice, it broke my heart. About the future, I saw many years of diligent effort to place the country in the level it once was. Not better, just the way it once was. I read once that "the people get the governments they deserve" and wondered: How did my people manage to produce such a bad governments? Where they that bad? Who was going to do the difficult task of reconstruction of the country? I had no answers for that.

My Little Venice, I never thought they would hurt you so much. Your own children tore your clothes and left you naked in the heavy rains of July. Abandoned after more than a century breastfeeding the dreams of all, shivering of cold, coughing your pneumonia, and which some hope could finally kill you.

You are no longer the same young girl that never aged, the Little Venice who raised me before letting me go out to face the world. The very one who showed her fair face with pride, and now looks down at the ground in shame with nothing to cover your bony body, and protect you from the skinny hungry dogs that lurk around you waiting for you to die, to finally chew on your bones.

"The Llanera Soul" has been lost. We are not and do not deserve to be "Brothers of the foam, or the heron, or the sun…" anymore.

I wish I had the will or time to write more about this, but it is too painful, I have to continue the trail…

***

Chapter 2

Alive is the only thing we really are. If a son could choose a mother, I would choose mine, again and again. Not because she was perfect, on the contrary, she had numerous limitations, but because she was unconditional.

That is to say, throughout her life she was happy when I was and inconsolable sad when I suffered. As if we were one, not two. Never I gave her proper credit and I regret that most of all. For that reason, when I think of past loves, this is the one that hurts the most, because was the one that deserved so much and the one that got less and I was most unfair with. She was my first and dearest love. Nothing can be done now. I wish she was here to at least read these words and have the satisfaction of knowing that above anyone else I love her and miss her.

Mother was a stoic woman of clear mind, firm believes and relentless actions. She had a sense of order and she was way optimistic, perhaps a little stubborn at times especially when she felt she was right and if the matter had to do with honor or people's welfare.

***

Exactly one year after the water buffalos came, I was conceived. And the man that became my father, by the miracle of love, was transformed into a most willing provider: everything, from goods and services to zealous protection. He was a good strong man who distributed his love and time between his buffaloes and his young family.

Mother became suddenly the object of infinite care. Her own merits enhanced by my imperceptible presence. Way before my time, things began to happen. Mother had to quit smoking, resume a healthy diet and assume moderate activities. No more horseback riding, jogging or gym routine. Biweekly check-ups were prescribed. A small crib dressed on lace and piles of diapers, hoodies, pajamas, socks and gloves where collected, obviously too early in time, and a little too big in size.

From time to time disagreements appeared regarding the choice of my name or whether my likeness would be more like my mother or my father. At that time grandma's opinion was not taken much into consideration, yet. This went on for months, while I grew and grew and grew. Then when least expected I became Facundo, the second generation of Facundo Marval.

Since I was born I was surrounded by happy people: Ma, Pa and grandma. There was always a lot of laughter. Back then, I learned that the only thing that can express more feelings than the written or spoken word is a good laugh and a warm hug.

Since the beginning, I was much more into my mother's feelings than she did ever know. I understood more clearly, what was not said tan what was said. I could read her thoughts, especially those that eventually would be written in her diary about what surrounded us...

> *"The sight of the mountain ridge and the feel of the downward cool breeze swirling from the north, mixed with the fragrance of the green pastures, the sight of the dandelions, and the peaceful murmurs of the mountain spring was intoxicating..."*

It all reminds me of you mother and how grateful I am to be your son and how much I love you and how sad I am I never told you. My mother and I simply lived in the same world. We understood each other, and that the heart speaks the only language that we truly, truly understand. Some call it love. My Ma taught me that language, early on through her gestures. We never spoke about it. My dear Mom and I depended psychologically on each other very much.

One time many years after, when I was a grown man in great distress, all I could think of and cry was: "I need my Ma, I need my Ma!"

It seems she came to my rescue, because immediately I felt renewed energy to hold on. Oh! How I regret not having given her the support, love and understanding, when she most needed it.

***

Then in 1944 my little sister came. Everything changed. The house, the ranch, the cows and the whole family took second place and everything began to revolve around her. I made up a little joke saying that she became the lady of the house taking mom's place and making everyone follow only her wishes.

We named her Isabel in honor of my Ma, because she was a picture perfect copy of her, right from her expressive eyes down to her little chubby toes, the second generation Isabel Marval. I was already three years old when this happened and for some reason, even at that early age, I felt directly responsible for her, even over my mother or father or grandma.

Chapter 3

Seven hundred kilometers from our town of El Dorado, was the Capital of the country. An amazingly beautiful valley, called "Santiago de Leon", separated from the sea by a massive mountain, "El Avila".

Early in the morning before the moist dew dried. The General - the dictator -, who had been ruling the country for thirty years, rode his black stallion around his personal pleasure grounds as usual. Two men responsible for his safety rode behind, close to him, but not too close to interfere with his sense of personal freedom. The briskly horse was particularly lively. That day he was in a pleasant mood and very optimistic about his resent decision to upgrade his cabinet with a more technocratic generation.

Daily, for one hour he rode across his private gardens and hunting grounds, before returning to have breakfast with his closest aids. Hot chocolate and churros was the day's fare, which everyone consumed in small portions trying to be very inconspicuous, because The General was very mindful about table manners. These preferred details gave him the sensation of high class upbringing and belonging to some elite, instead of his real rough humble beginning. To him this was an important matter of self-esteem.

In Little Venice most dictators sprang from a group of the third grade bullies, who grew up, enrolled in the military, eventually became generals, and with their comrades, terrorized the nation, robed the treasure chests of the state, all in the name of a revolution that never existed, making people poorer and destroying their self-esteem, general after general, generation after generation…

The General was just one more pseudo revolutionary with an autocratic style of leadership. He made himself believe he was conducting a justifiably and real war, in protection of the lower classes from the bourgeois, although the reasoning for this war was only a product of his imagination. He did not understand the role of the job creation class. In doing so, he drove investors to nil, destroyed the job offer and in an effort to substitute these allies, militarized civil service. The result was disastrous: shortage of goods and services, unemployment, currency devaluation, astronomical inflation, in short total chaos.

He was convinced that nothing was entirely false or entirely true, and he constantly took advantage of that ambiguity. He knew that in the history of mankind, nothing had been proven absolutely, and constantly justified his failures by blaming a convenient scape goat, "The rich".

Contradictory, everything had been proven relatively clearly already and he knew it. Anyone could be right or wrong at times and when it becomes obvious that one is wrong, should admit it and change course, because anything could be possible under the right circumstances.

It became easier for him to interpret other people than himself and he enjoyed digging deeply into their minds, as if he was searching for the answers he did not have. Inspiration was *"A flor de piel"* like the Spaniards say, because pseudo revolutionaries are everywhere.

Many colors were needed to describe The General, because he had the ability to change like a Chameleon according to the political weather. This generated passionate feelings, for and against his persona. The challenge here was not to separate what could be real from what could not, or what happened against what did not, because anything was possible. After all, reality outdoes fiction all the time. Nothing can be more unbelievable that reality and that was the way it was then.

He thought of himself as a Liberator, the person who facilitated the actions of people to be freed from oppressors, who did not allow them to achieve their own destine in life. Promoting class differences to perpetuate his domination, The General sadly became the oppressor. When everybody is at fault justice can't be served. That was the state of affairs.

I am still saddened for all the misery, the hunger and the persecution prevalent at that time, as always due to a single reason: greed. Fortunately, controversial views make people think and make decisions and choose. Eventually they will...

***

One of the two ways to rank a country is by how efficient the postal service is and how compassionately the country treats immigrants.

If the letters and packages arrive on time and do not get lost on the way, it is a very good indicator that the country runs well. It demonstrates that the people have respect for each other and are civilized. The assurance that the mail is not being tampered with increases people's trust. Ideas, dreams and opportunities flow on the rails of the Postal System. During The General's mandate the mail was intercepted, censored and finally lost!

Immigrants, on the other hand, are the only people in the world, who by choice are where they want to be. Not by circumstance or by force - free. No matter where they come from they pay a dear price: The nostalgia for the old country left behind. A country is the foundation upon which all families stand; if it fails, everyone is doomed! During The General's mandate there were no immigrants. That was the state of affairs in Little Venice.

***

A miserable human being, with a stitched scar on his recently shaved head, who spent his life scavenging in the deepest rat holes, together with a similar partner, choked, robed and left a man dead in the middle of the darkness on the way to El Dorado. Took his pickup truck to the nearest chop shop to be dismantled and sold it for parts.

Three days later we found out, when the police arrived at our door, the deceased man was my father, the first generation Facundo Marval. He bled to death in the middle of a torrential rain and eventually was incidentally discovered by two horseback riders passing through.

The whole system was rotting under The Generals very own feet and I lost my father, similar actions were being perpetrated by common criminals, politicians and businessman alike, in a society that simply did not understand.

***

This tragedy changed our lives. It happened in March two months before I turned nine and my little sister six. Ma decided right there and then that she did not want to see us grow under such a horrific estate of affairs and took immediate steps to sell the ranch in order to get away as far as we possibly could.

The destination of choice, after a brief stopover in grandma's apartment in the capital, was Miami, Florida, a place where many people with dreams either went or wanted to go. It broke grandma's heart to find out that after so many years of love and hard work, the water buffalo ranch only fetched thirty thousand dollars, counting all the land, the white house, the rose garden, every act of love and every single horn.

Ma invited grandma to join us on the trip and help her take care of us kids, while she broke ground. Grandma argued that just the change of air, not to mention the language, would kill her. Deep inside, we knew that in her case that was probably true. Some people can't be separated from their roots.

She further argued and insisted that if she went far away, who will take the trouble, from time to time, to go to El Dorado and water the lawn and place fresh flowers on her son's grave? She was not wrong, there was no one else left. But how do you explain to a grieving grandma, that the greenest lawn and the freshest flowers are grown in the deepest layer of soil of your very own soul, under perpetual water and the brightest sun. Impossible!

Instead she proposed that baby Isabel could stay with her, until things cleared up for us. To reinforce the idea she explained that Isabel was only six years old and very adaptable and that it was not the first time a grandma would come to the rescue in case of emergencies. Just to hear the idea made us shiver, but at the time we could not think of any other solution.

So we spent a week in grandma's arranging all the travel documents and parted, knowing full well that it was going to take some time before we would see Isabel and grandma again. Grandma hugged Ma and then me, the only way she knew how to express love and tenderness. With a good laugh and a warm hug! Then she whispered a little hush secret in Ma's ear.

Later, sitting in the plane I asked mother what was it grandma said to her ear? "I want to be buried in the niche besides Facundo, my son." Mother responded.

***

Once we arrived at Miami's airport, we were taken to a special cubicle, where not-properly documented aliens were screened. There we argued our case in terms of the extreme psychological hardship we had to endure while we lived under the regime of The General and pleaded, on compassionate grounds, to let us stay. We did not complied with the asylum regulations of the time, because "our life was not in danger", which was probably true in the short term.

As a last resort we invoked my father's incident as an example of what was waiting for us there. To what they argued, that a criminal act like that could happen anywhere in the world and was not the result of political targeting. We did not qualified and were ordered to return.

I still live with the impression that the immigration officer that processed our case had sympathy on us and was on our side, but his hands were tied on a roll of wick like a kite entangled in the electricity lines. Many years later, it has been recognized that widespread dangerous conditions in a region, where grounds to grant eligibility and grant people the status of "refuge".

***

As mother later commented in her diary:

"We found ourselves in the biggest predicament of our lives. It was clear we had to leave Miami next day, but to come right back to the country we were fleeing from, was a devastating way to accept failure. Our lives would be destroyed, if we didn't at least try to put up a good fight. But where else could we go? That is when the idea of stopping over Cuba came to my mind. After all, the flight from Miami to Santiago de Leon made a quick stop in Havana…"

Mother discussed it with me and I said, "Why not, we have never been in Havana. People say is nice there."

My words of encouragement were enough for her to recover new energy, for both of us to continue our fight for survival. We made arrangements with the Airline and soon enough found ourselves taking an evening walk pampered by the warm breeze of the "Malecon de la Havana".

After, mother and son settled themselves into a modest class, middle of the road, non-tourist hostel and were then now searching for a warm bowl of soup and bread as an evening meal. Murmuring to each other with honest great hopes, "Tomorrow is another day…"

***

The following day, with the optimistic high energies of great fighters, we settled to a cup of coffee while browsing the morning paper for a quick job. The greater forces of nature help those who try hard in search of a just cause. Mom was hired as a chamber maid and I as an assistant bellboy at the Tropicana Hotel of all places. Nothing like starting at a humble position, in a more than famous establishment, to teach humility to the most arrogant of souls!

We took our new beginning gracefully and communicated the good news to grandma in a very melancholic letter. Highlighting how grateful we were to Cuba for opening an unexpected door for us, to continue our journey after such a terrible turn around. Expressing our wishes for grandma and Isabel's health and welfare, hoping to be reunited as soon as the circumstances allowed it…

***

The circumstances did not allow it, the days, the months and the years passed by. Eighteen years! General, after General, after General…We who were relatively young at the time of departure (Mom twenty nine, grandma forty nine, Isabel six and me nine) had grown older. Isabel became so attached to grandma, that at the time of grandma's passing she loved her more that her own mother and under no circumstance would consider leaving the country. Grandma was buried according to her will, besides her son Facundo at El Dorado's cemetery.

We kept Isabel company for two weeks. During the visit we found out that Isabel was engaged to be married, kept a steady job as a nurse in Santiago de Leon, had a social group and a very fulfilling life altogether. Logically she was the only beneficiary in grandma's will. Mom and I concluded that the outcome of Isabel's life was a direct consequence of our decision to live her behind. Time sweep so fast, that we didn't realized we were losing part of our family. Oblivious of the harm we were causing…

II - The Duchess

Goodbye my dear friend
Never to see you again
My heart has worn out and failed
From loving too hard too much
Better too hard and much than none at all
Better dead than alive without you my friend

Goodbye my dear friend
Never to see you again
Thanks for the companionship
Thanks for the understanding
My heart has worn out and failed
From so much tenderness and care

Better this way than never
Better suffering than in peace without you my dear friend…

Chapter 4

At that time I used to nickname everything. Cats, dogs, horses and anything else that moved. Her real name was Marilu, but I nicknamed her "The Duchess". Come to think of it, because it sounded right and maybe because this description looked a lot like her. She stood very distinguished, slender, carried a languished gaze which gave her kind of a royal air and freedom to move around as she pleased.

Generally in the earlier days she was fun to be with, often playful, seldom sad, her overall appearance to the world, one of a happy lady. And also because one day she told me she would marry a "Prince" and I thought myself sort of a little prince too. She was definitely a princess, behaved like one, and expected everyone to recognize her as such.

We first crossed paths in Habana Cuba around 1951, when she and her father moved to the house next door to ours, where I lived with my mother. I was ten, she was seven. At that time I was not much interested in girls and ignored her totally until she was ten and I thirteen, when suddenly we appeared to have something in common to talk about.

Around that time the first thing we noticed was that my mother and her father did have more than a causal acquaintance and often talked while watering the plants of the tiny gardens that fronted our houses. Each one on their side of their fence at the beginning, then they began to come to each other's house for occasional coffee. Later on often on for a night or two a month, to listen to the music and sip wine at the bar around the corner. We didn't know anything else, but that was enough to call our attention and make us start our own friendship.

She confided in me not ever remembering having a mother or any details about her, since her father refused to talk about it or even pronounced her name.

We concluded that she had probably had done him very wrong and hurt him in some deep unforgiving way, for him to behave that way and dismiss her altogether. She probably ran off with another man.

The Duchess pointed out at that time that she was ready to forgive her because she missed her so much. She pointed out truly that everyone deserves to have a mother. She even said that at times, when she looked at herself in the mirror, she imagined looking a little like her mother and played slight variations in her nostalgic way.

I agreed wholeheartedly with her, because I also missed my father very much. Even though I knew for certain that he left us and was buried in El Dorado, sometimes I imagined us crossing paths. My mother constantly was saying good things about him and how much he used to love us in his own way. Mothers usually do that, because they don't want us to grow up with resentments in our hearts, because they know it would hurt us even more.

The Duchess' father himself was a fine silk and other fine fabric merchant from Damascus, who ended up in Cuba as a last resort. Because also at the last moment out of the boat he was not let into de United States and had no money to return all the way back

Eventually after performing a myriad of odd jobs in Cuba, he was able to save enough money, use his contacts within the trade, import fabrics into the country and open his own shop, at a time when fortunately ladies, or their seamstresses, made their own dresses. He prospered.

His shop was a few blocks from our houses, very conveniently located within walking distance. At that time my mother worked as a telegraphist at the post office and often on took turns with The Duchess' father to walk us kids to school.

Time passed through elementary and high school. The Duchess and I progressed from best friends, to sweet hearts and eventually to steady boy and girl friend.

On the day of my high school prom in 1958, I took The Duchess as my very own, very special date. She wore a best quality chiffon pearl color gown, made especially for her by my mom and the best fabric her father could find at the store. That evening I placed my graduation ring on her finger and promised to love her "Forever". I was seventeen and she was fourteen.

By that time The Duchess, her father, my Ma and me where family. The one neither of us ever had before, but still lived next door to each other.

***

The next few years brought deep and wide changes. It was 1959. Fidel Castro and his milicianos descended from the mountains and overthrew the government regime of Fulgencio Batista. The powerful dictator, permanently dressed in his white linen suit, fled to the Dominican Republic.

From then on, Cuba changed forever and eventually my Ma and I were forced to reevaluate our footing. The dilemma became: to stay under the rapidly changing communist political system or move to Miami protected under our changed status and stablish ourselves there.

It was not an easy choice, because my Ma was already head deep sentimentally involved with the Duchess' father and I with The Duchess. My mother exhausted herself trying to convince them, that to leave was not desirable but very convenient for all of us. Her opinion was that we did not have to take it, and we should move to Miami and start a new life away from the extremely controlling circumstances.

Immediately we became divided by an ideology of extreme nationalism. The father and The Duchess decided to stay, because above all they considered themselves "Cubans". On the contrary mother and I decided to leave, because we saw ourselves, above all as "Individuals", who deserve to be happy. They simply considered us selfish and not loyal to the country and the cause and the revolution…

So called socialist revolutions seemed to persecute us everywhere we went. For the second time in our lives we had to consider exiling ourselves to maintain our personal liberties and try to live in peace.

This debate lasted five years, during which I managed to go through medical school and The Duchess through high school. The denouement finally came in 1964.

What is one supposed to do? Be loyal to one's adopted country and the preferences of the loved ones and in doing so be dissatisfied with oneself the rest of one life, or flee. We fled and soon enough found us living in a rented room in Little Havana, Mother working in Bloomindale's and me as a nurse in the Hialeah Hospital. We wrote back to Cuba every week pleading for a little understanding and lenience towards the dream of being together once more. Time proved it was of no use. From then on we all pretended to continue to live next door of each other for the next ten years, even though we were miles away.

***

Civil liberties diminished greatly in Cuba and the country was heavily subsidized by the Soviet Union with no signs of reversal. It was 1974. We tried once more to convince our two loves left behind, to come to us, at no avail. By this time I managed to validate my medical credentials and was recognized as a full medical doctor in the state of Florida. I was thirty three. Mother was already fifty three and closer to retirement from her job at Bloomindale's. Neither of us had considered any other sentimental solutions to our lives, except the possibilities that the "dear neighbors next door" would change their minds and would eventually come to live with us.

I personally urged the duchess to convince her father, who was already sixty three, to move with her to Florida, under our sponsorship, he refused. I could not comprehend the reasons for his stubbornness, since he was not even a Cuban national (He always refused to give up his original citizenship), could not really speak fluently the language and the country financially speaking had not been particularly generous to him, on the contrary, things where very tight. Some aliens can be more nationalistic towards their adopted county than the National Anthem! He was one of them.

We went through good, bad and worse times for a long, long time, together. This said a lot about her and me because after so many ups and downs, someone else would have given up and parted ways long ago. Not us we stocked it out. Eventually we did, because it seems that everything is less than eternal. Nevertheless our lives collided often on, also for a long, long time.

"I don't have anybody to talk to about these things".

She used to say apologetically, every time she called me at Miami, from Cuba. I didn't expect to be of much help, especially considering that I didn't have the best of heads at that time, but apparently she thought I would.

"Okay I will listen uninterruptedly, even if it takes an hour and then I will give you my opinion."

And I listened and listened and listened… When I felt she didn't have anything more to say, because she began to sob, then I would tell her:

"Look Duchess, life does not behave the way we wish. The world does not revolve around us. We are the ones that have to adjust to every situation, otherwise we make it harder."

"But…"

She insisted, because she always had to have the last word!

"You may think otherwise but it will not change things" I would say.

By the time she realized I was not going to please her wishes, blaming other souls for her misfortunes, she then concluded it was time to change the subject and end the call. But most of the time I was given news about her, via common acquaintances, which ratified how stubborn she could be at times.

***

Many times I told The Duchess to think about our future together in Florida, but her answer was categorical "I will never leave my father behind". That I understood, because I knew that if I was placed in the same predicament, I would also never leave mother behind. This loyal quality has kept us separated so far.

The following year I received an urgent call from The Duchess telling me that her father was terminally ill at the hospital and asking if I was willing to be with her and him in his final moments. After all, she said, I was the only person that she could think to be with her in such a moment. We were the only family she ever had. I was not really able, but I could not refuse. Mother insisted she would also come.

We arrived at the intensive care unit in the hospital and as soon as we got there a nurse rushed us to The Duchess' father room, saying "I sure hope we make it on time". The Duchess was standing at her father's side holding his slender hand, when I whispered to her "Here we are…" She looked at me and then at mother and then at the old man. Without saying a word he expired shortly after and was taken away. He was 70. He didn't suffer much.

Later, during our conversation at the cafeteria, the Duchess informed us that it was her father's wish not to have a funeral as such, except our presence during the cremation ceremony. Next day everything was arranged and done as he wanted it. All and all we stayed a week, at The Duchess' house and took time to review the neighborhood.

During our walks many memories came back.

After the week was over we left for Miami, mother to her retiree house routine and taking care of me and I to my hospital duties. At the airport, when I embraced The Duchess for the last time, I was tempted to remind her that my permanent invitation to come and join me in Miami was always standing, but at the end I did not considered the time and the place appropriate because of the resent events.

On the way home on the plane, I asked mother how many times had she tried in the past to convince the Duchess' father to move to Miami with her and she answered, "countless". "You see Facundo, some people are rigid about some things and that was one of his ways. To them it is not a negotiable matter, even if their life depended on it. Us, we have to learn to live without them, I have done it, and I had no choice. Now it is all in the past, just history..." I wondered if the Duchess inherited that characteristic from her father also.

***

As soon as I caught up with my duties at the hospital, I wrote The Duchess a brief letter,

Dear Marilu:

In spite of the sad circumstances that brought us all together this time, I was glad to be near you once more. Mother and I commented, that from time to time life gives us the opportunity to discover, once more, what is dear to us.

I must say that you occupy that place in my heart. The question remains: What are we going to do about it? During all these years it has been so clear to me that mother belonged with your father and you belong with me. Nature went to extremes to place us in the same path. I think it is time to recognize that fact. Now that your father has left us, I do not see any reason to prevent you from coming to Miami and join mother and me.

I am so certain that this is meant for us, that I think we should go through our wedding vows shortly after you arrival.

I know this outcome would have pleased your father and certainly we have mother's blessing to accompany us. Please give this proposal your most serious attention and please be aware that it would make me the happiest person on earth,

Yours ever loving,

Facundo

Two weeks went by and I did not receive any answer from The Duchess. I was by then sure that she was struggling with my proposal, but why? She was now free to choose without any further considerations or impediment. But the human soul has many strange ways of dealing with identical circumstances.

I was required to make some sense of the whole thing on behalf of her and myself. I didn't know how but someone had to do it. I was the newly appointed puzzle solver and besides I was the man, always expected to find the way. Our lives continued regardless, at a distance, but continued.

***

. Once Isabel, my sister, wrote me a letter covering the years of absence which had passed since grandma passed away. Luckily, she continued to be happily married, and was the mother of two fine teenagers, a boy and a girl. Sadly, she reported that the country has gone from bad to worse, particularly regarding safety, since crime has gone out of control. Economically also very bad since the currency has become almost worthless and people resorted to swapping and trading as a way to go around it. The government has lost control of every conceivable aspect of public administration, and remains in power by force, sustained only by the support of the army who pledges alliance in exchange for bribes.

Personally they had followed the same path that father laid and are running a little farm near El Dorado of all places, which gives them enough to live on, and have a certain degree of independence. God bless them and have pity on my dear Little Venice.

***

Seventeen years have passed. I was calling from Miami Florida and I haven't spoken to The Duchess for more than two years now. Not because we didn't try but because we failed to communicate every time. What was happening right now was the result of bad handling of a series of petty little mishaps, which had grown into mountains of grudges. When we were little The Duchess and I were very close. We hanged to each other while climbing our difficulties, but eventually she grew up and turned to strangers for help.

The one she chose, Feliciano Madrid, was a scoundrel. He owned land just for the sake of it. A "saltinbanquen" (bank robber), one may say, who inherit his titles without earning a bit. He sported an old leathery skin and whitened hair and looked like he lived forever already. During his life he profited from that land without doing a thing, only selling or leasing mostly fraudulent rights. This was the bad weed The Duchess allowed to grow in her garden.

The truth is usually as elusive as a panther threading through the midnight pitch dark jungle, blending its yellow and black patches of fur, against the greenish-black-blue of the humid and foggy forest. Whatever we manage to think it is, it is not, even though is there. Did this really happen? Only the jungle of our subconscious minds knows.

***

There were only thirty six miles from the island of Cuba to the Florida mainland and a few more from Habana to Miami, but the philosophical differences of The Duchess and I, placed us at an astronomical distance away. Personally I found her out of reach even though I tried to understand.

To be able to negotiate those differences took more courage than all the water of the stretch of sea one had to cross. What made it even harder was the knowledge that doing so, could radically change you, your life, and perhaps reach a point of no return. That was frightening.

The question was not how good the person you left behind is, but how much love is left behind and how much you miss each other. At the end, whatever is done - based on that - cannot be undone.

As I learned later she was very sick, terminally ill with a cancer that was eating her alive. She decided not to tell me in order to use the sickness to end her suffering and spare mine. Once I thought about doing the same thing to exonerate my family and me of the horrors of death and instead decided to write a sweet farewell letter to each one, explaining my decision, as an act of compassion when my time came along.

But people change their minds. I did and so did her, on the basis that silence at the end did not do justice to anyone, because souls are expected to say something, because it would be the last opportunity and the spoken words will defeat time. So, eventually I received a phone call from The Duchess, not asking but begging for me to be at her side before she passed away.

I was grateful for her request and extremely sad for the reasons of it. At the end I went and it was a good decision, because death has to be tackled right on by those in it and those connected to them in any way. This is one of the most elementary rules of life. The time does not allow for indecision.

***

"So how are you Duchess?" I asked her after a brief silence while we gazed at each other's eyes waiting for a reaction, any kind of reaction.   .

"I am alright" she said.

"I still know who and where I am, and I know where I am soon going to be" she said.

"Where are you going Duchess?" I asked as if I was not aware.

"Nowhere" she said with a tear dropping down her chick. "I know we don't go anywhere."

It was Christmas1991 and I was 50. Whenever The Duchess was sick it always happened in December, she had no control over it, it simply was her season. Death is a sneaky thing…

***

I believe in change, progressive change. Similarly I don't believe in revolutions, especially those conducted in the name of the people. Soon these demagogic movements serve as platforms for other elites, bringing greater faults. Progressive change is the main rule of life. I am amazed how some people are reluctant to accept this main principle of nature, missing out the little joys of living with ease, and the opportunity to die in peace taken by the flow. Still, the only real value and answer to everything is love.

***

The next day being a holyday I had a slow start, trying to reconcile things. Eventually I decided to drop by Joe's Bar, the neighborhood home away from home, the place were those of us who have no friends go to validate life and get an opinion. Especially when one is not so clear minded and the subject of our worries is not so tangible, trusting that a drink or two will clear things up.

The bottles were stacked like led soldiers, in perfect formation. The bar had been catering to the same neighborhood for fifty years. Not counting the two that it operated under a different name, before Joe bought it in 1947, two years after the war, then it was called *"El Encuentro"*. First he changed the name to *"Joe's Bar"*; to send a clear message that there he was the boss. Then he renovated the two washrooms and padded the chairs, on the premise that people come to a bar mainly to drink, and then have the urge to pee, but also to feel comfortable when they sit to talk.

Besides that, nothing else was changed, since the days my Ma used to go there with The Duches' father, even the dust remained, reason why Joe's started to attract an older crowd curious to find out if there was a real Joe behind the bar and if he was a good listener. You could tell that one by one of the customers became regulars, because they found a real Joe behind the bar and he was a good listener. Some on fixed days, others when they wanted to feel welcome somewhere. For me it was already time to go home. At the end the revolution had won, and us, poor us, we didn't have a chance at love…

***

When I arrived back at Miami Ma could notice the deep sorrow in the creases of my face. Before she could asked me anything

> I said,
> "She passed away peacefully"
> "Thank goodness, more suffering at the end is no justification for hanging on longer"

For me it was like closing up half a century of my life, because I always felt I was living for her all along, no matter how distant we ended up being.

Around that time mother and I moved to the little town of Hollywood, north of Miami, where Ma could enjoy a more peaceful retirement and I could have a smaller town atmosphere to dedicate myself progressively more and more to my writing, and less and less to the medical practice. After all, my golden trail had provided me with plenty to say. I had, by then, become an authority in the art of storing feelings in little compartments; to eventually let them out in writing like freeing little doves at the right time, one at a time.

Chapter 5

On that Christmas evening of 1992 I was alone. Mother had retired for the night already. I was sitting in my favorite velvet chair, my legs stretched upon the matching futon, my red sock clad feet lined towards the chimney. I was trying to reread Nabokov's memoir *'Speak, Mind'*, but couldn't. My own mind wondered around the barely lighten purple room, forcing me to glimpse at a distant past.

It was a forest, dense, humid and hot, sliced by a large serpent like river, which of all the places known to me resembled the Amazon. My spirit was dragging me south. I always wanted to run away from those bearings. My desire had always been to fly high and north, not low and south. It didn't make sense.

By then I was familiar with the unusual, which often disguises its unique peculiar forms this way. I sensed I had unfinished business and an urge to resolve it. We all have unresolved issues from the past, from time to time, but no practical way to deal with them. I put the though aside and retired for the night…

The next morning I decided to call my sister. It has been already one year since The Duchess passing and I needed to talk to somebody, besides Ma.

"Mrs. Isabel is not home", the maid said. Aware that I could hear the commands she was being told. "And if he calls again tell him I am gone on a long trip", I heard Isabel said. The maid repeated her words and did not make any effort to muzzle her orders. She knew this was a habit her Mrs. had. Since her youth, anytime she wanted people to know they were not welcome she would do the same thing. It was Isabel's way of handling her own reality, always through other people. I do not recall a time, during our adult life, that I actually spoke directly "to her", not "through her", "by her" or "around her".

She was easy to get offended because inside of her was this tiny little person always afraid…

There is a child within each one of us, who refuses to grow. Who only appears at times of extreme solitude or tribulation, at those times when we feel that we had been pierced at the deepest?

Unguarded and afraid, but nevertheless this little person dares to come out of the safe depth of our soul, to help, and we feel her presence with amazement, during that much needed dialog, which perhaps lasts a few seconds but it means everything…Like any little person at that time we could look up to our mother, god or the greater forces of nature for help, and most of the time we would get it.

***

I didn't get offended at all. On the contrary, it messaged me that somehow without knowing or even wanting, I had hurt her once more, one more time since we left her behind with grandma. For what I was truly sorry, and for what I had to pay once again. As I have done hundreds of times before. You see I know her quite well, because once, a long time ago now, she was my sister.

I hanged up the phone, grabbed my brief case and umbrella and went about my business of teaching Psychology at Miami University. That morning I gave the example of Isabel, as a dependent manipulative personality, who must use others to relate to the environment. Unwillingly to do it herself, and forced to master manipulation to the level of art. Texts books say that this personality comes to be, when someone is treated impersonally as a child, that is, like an object. Brought up not at all like a loving human, but more like a "doll" sitting or standing just there…

Past the example, we moved to a dissertation about the scheduled term paper. The psychology of love, under two premises: Is love an egocentric need for attention? Is it an exocentric drive for wellbeing? In other words, is true love "receiving" or "giving?"

And I finish saying "A little bit below the heart are the things we do not tell anyone, that is where the real stories lie. Mostly dreams about what we wish out of life, mostly things that have not become true yet. Once they become reality they are moved to a different place within: the good and bad memories room.

I must have said something brilliantly right, because the higher forces of nature rewarded me with a relatively peaceful day dedicated mainly to this dilemma.

At the end of the day I reached a non-scholastic conclusion of love. I said to myself: "You know my friend what love really is? Well I will tell you, love is when you are in need of a small transplant piece of liver, to be able to continue living and one person is willing to give it to you. That person loves you!" The disappointing truth is that almost no one would be willing to do that much for you, no matter how much they think they love you…

***

My sister and I, as far as I can remember, were always very close. That is, after I left her with grandma and soon after she married, when we drifted far, far away. It was always a state of mind, not based on any specific event, she would say. As well, by implicit agreement we decided (many years ago) not to include Ma in this controversial subject. Isabel insisted in blaming me entirely for everything bad that happened regardless and exonerated Ma, because it would had only make her life miserable during her later years, which we agreed was inhuman. So, for years, Isabel blamed me exclusively and this allowed her and Ma to correspond undisturbed.

By virtue of that agreement, I also had to assume the role of older brother at a young age, which I not always exercised to her approval. Nevertheless she still trusted me for a while to guide the way and silently followed, even though it was obvious I didn't always know where to turn. This fact appeared so obvious later on, when our roles switched. She became more enlighten and I more obscure…

"I am sorry. You may blame me for everything that happened or everything that didn't happen. I did the only thing I could do." I said to her once, in what it seemed to me was a logical explanation, but not to her. I didn't convince her at all, I mean not at all…

Eventually, I lost myself in a sea of letters and words, which I barely understood myself, because I was foreign to the meaning of them, but they sounded well and followed the sweet notes, I became a letter writer. I suddenly could think, dream, speak and write, and become relatively happy again, mending patches in the weave of my life.

I mainly wrote about myself in my letters to her, I had no other reference between us. I set and described myself as an example of what can and can't be achieved in life, almost apologizing for being who I was.

***

Dear Isabel:

I could have been anything, because apparently I had many talents. Only I didn't choose right. I spent the majority of my life practicing at being, not being. I could have been generally anything related to the arts. Instead I became a medical doctor, a psychiatrist of all things! Of course my past was unfulfilled...

At the end I became as valuable as the circumstances allowed me. I was tied to their will. My personality would not allow me to work towards a purpose of my own. I was compelled to do it always thinking about someone else, as if I alone didn't count or even existed.

A great sense of guilt came over me just thinking that I could own or enjoy something without sharing it with someone else. It became a requisite to be tied constantly to those who were supposed to love me. It was not only the rejection of ones ideas in terms of a word or two. It had to do with the total misconception of who one was. This was enough to make you want to shout "I am not like that!

It became a life of deprivation mostly from the absence of peace and security, rather than plain not having. I grew up being barely middle class in every respect. Doing without some things was our way, and it made us carry the heavy load of being pretentious, educated and poor, simultaneously. However it brought an additional benefit when the time came, I could also be generous, humble and strong.

So after more than thirty years of living like this, I still don't know if I was the most stupid person or on the contrary the most versatile persons ever. Separately, I mastered the art of conversation and writing. I could write or speak all day and never say a word. I know it is hard for you to understand. I didn't want to be just a farmer, but I didn't want to be just a doctor, what I really wanted to be deep inside was just a writer...
Love you dearly,

Facundo

***

Eventually, Isabel (my sister) decided not to see me or speak to me again. Even though, life is too short and nor she or I have much time left to live. She says, I remind her of my father's, my mother's, mine and her own failures, all at the same time, which was too much for her to bear. An immense loss for both of us, if you ask me, to break so dramatically for such an undefined matter, in my opinion much greater than the pain she would have experienced if she decided to see me.

I kept calling her from time to time, regardless. And invariably the maid would respond, "Ms. Isabel is not home, she has gone on a long trip…"

I wish this never happened.

***

Chapter 6

In Hollywood, Florida, folks go to church on Sunday and from time to time confess little sins. Not like the ones that took place daily, but enough to keep the parish priest busy. The small town is one of the stops on route, where the passengers of the greyhound bus to Atlanta take a rest on the bones and one deserved bacon on toast sandwich. The bus stop has only two rooms; one for the waiting passengers and the snack bar, and the other one for the ticket counter and washrooms.

Jody Johnson publisher of the Hollywood Review had a hard time printing local news, because nothing happened in Hollywood, aside from the death and birth notices, and every few years a visit from an aspiring governor candidate. The town votes republican on its majority and is almost southern Roman Catholic in its entirety.

Reginald Coles, a Jesuit priest kept his time equally divided between his rose garden, the church and Sunday Bible School behind the church's graveyard, which meant roughly 2.3333 days a week devoted to each.

After The Duchess passed away, for some strange reason her memory filled entirely my soul, not leaving room for any other living being except Ma. I concentrated my intellectual interest on the philosophical controversies that I could find around me, with the hope that they could serve as material topics for my future books.

***

"That is a shame Jody Johnson". Reginald Coles said. "How can you say such a thing? That is the truth. The matters of the church must be taken literally, not reasoned. Anything else is heretic!"

Which Jody Johnson replied, "I think man created god urged to materialize a super being. Really all we had to do was to look up at the universe to find it."

***

This was the type of things that were discussed at the time. An editorial duel around subjects like this went on for years. Jody Johnson would write on her editorial space and Reginal Coles will respond on his weekly column and his Sunday mass pulpit. By virtue of this clash of opinions many people, as well as myself, now understand less: not only what happened, but why it happened and the significance of every event debated.

By this time I had become a full time writer and I started to think more. I also learned that there is not such a thing as mistakes. The choices are made and each choice brings consequences, totally unrelated to the concept of right or wrong. Nobody is at fault in the development of one's ideas, until proven wrong.

For example, when animals get hurt they lie down, lick their wounds and rest, and if the time comes to part, they drop their heads to the ground and wait, until they slowly vanish from this life. We don't, we fight to stay alive. A fight that is sometimes useless, often futile, and always lost.

All and all, the above reasoning entitles me to prove true that "The greatest masterpiece of all is a life well lived." But what do you do with a small life? The least you can do is to live every little piece to the fullest. Some people were awarded with lives larger than life, but sadly, often seldom manage to live them. They act them, simulate them, go through them in accordance to a script, but never lived them! This happens often among those devoted to creative lives.

I have done mine by instinct, no syllables, no scripts, but very much impromptu. In spite of all this reality and the fact that I have never had too many people within my circle, everyone seemed to have a clearly written story for me to follow, which I could not allow myself to perform. I could not act my life. Instead I followed my codes of destiny, mistake after mistake and all…That is how some of my most profound disagreements began. I just wanted the truth as it was, not as I wanted it to be. That was my religion.

In my literary quest, I decided to move into more transcendental subjects. I began searching for an answer to the question which had been in my mind for a long time: What is the purpose of life?

I realized that to give any kind of answer, I had to shed some light first into the purpose of my own life. I discovered that as we near the end of our lives, we care more about the fundamental, important and necessary, leaving the trivialities somehow behind. Considering this, I could not have chosen a better subject or a better moment…

Somewhere I read that as humans consumed more proteins, our brain grew from the size of a walnut, to a peach, to an orange, to a small watermelon, and developed the ability to assign meaning to events. We became more creative and curious, but also complicated, and developed a tendency to glorify concepts to make us feel important, which otherwise were simple matters.

Even though we are not, we still feel as if we are the center of everything. We are important regardless, but not that important. We don't need to look better. Imagination could be accepted as truth, because everything, and more, is possible!

For example, let us put aside all previous beliefs and become a "Thinker" for a moment. You do not need knowledge, just common sense, because the facts are here and now in front of us. I do not expect you to agree with my point of view. However, it would be beneficial to keep an open mind, in order to take advantage of the element of simplicity, which, we should try our earnest to keep handy at all times. Most things that appear extremely complex are in essence very simple, because that is the way nature works.

The truth is, since the beginning we didn't understand some aspects about life, so we made up stories to deliver quick answers to such unexplained subjects. This was possible because our brain was now large and possessed the ability to reason, be creative and assign meaning, and at the time science was unable to give us reasonable answers. This was practical and convenient and filled a temporary need.

But it did not accomplish other purpose, aside from temporarily calming our curiosity and our obsession about understanding. But it distorted simple facts, and created mystery around them. Grant you, the concepts became much more dramatic than real and made us look like problem solvers. We grew to a level of sophistication and glamour never achieved before.

Just to give an example: Was it necessary to define God as three persons in one? Clearly it was not a harmless misconception, compared to the fact that three fourths of humanity go without clean water and remain hungry. That is a fact which threatens our very own existence. Famine harvests sickness, which eventually could exterminate us all...

However, among all this neglect, some of us have chosen to live in relative comfort, which is not bad in itself, if it wasn't for the fact that the purpose of life has been totally left behind. Are we prepared to mend such a gross negligence, without threats or lies and only for the sake of truth? We better, because our own survival depends on it.

What does it matter if we are all going to die anyway? That is true from the point of view of an individual and I don't know if you are aware that it is also true collectible. It is a certainty that the solar system will explode, when our sun finally consumes itself.

But the amount of time until that ending is so large, that it will be stupid not to do something. It has taken us four and one halve million years, to come from a non-walking ape, hanging from a limb, to drive a Porsche on our way to our Apple computer.

But, before we had any record of being around, dinosaurs reined undisputedly the earth for one hundred and sixty million years!

Supposing we still have to live an equivalent amount of time, would it not make sense to review the purpose of our lives? And if we find, our purpose is to endure as a specie, live collectible according to that cannon. Putting aside wealth for a moment and accepting the fact that wealth does not buy health or happiness.

***

Suddenly I realized that my thinking was taking me right back to the opening statement of this book:

"Everyone has a golden trail laid out for them. We tend to think that it starts when we are born, but sometimes it's a continuation of our ancestor's. No matter what we do or don't, we will inevitably end up with it, because it's our one and only life. At a point in his life Facundo Marval, my father, wrote these prophetic words, which opened the written statement of a visionary dream that spearheaded to a place way far in the future..."

"And life went through me like a ray of light leaving very little behind and I was totally replaced. Only two generations had passed and I have been already forgotten, as well as millions before me. I am sad because my life has come and gone so soon, but glad because I have lived it and know life will continue for many others after me. It is our destiny...The grandson of my grandson, who had since then also disappeared, was reading a virtual digest magazine. I was long gone..."

Without knowing I had come back to the basis of my father's personal mind revolution and felt compelled to continue what he started, in my own way. I went back and read the whole passage again and discovered that he had a clear view about creating a new world, only by means of the revolution of the mind.

He professed that we would only be civilized if we did away with the differences created by greed.

I found a new purpose within my commitment to writing, because believe me, words are the most powerful tool of transformation. This purpose became my new found passion or you may say my "new love".

***

III – Mount Pleasant

When I am no more
Will you still love me?
And be the keeper of my memories
And the little black box where my ashes rest.

From time to time miss me?
And our walks in the park
And our talks over tea

About life
About love
About death

And when you are about to shed a tear
Always remember that you promised not to cry
And be the keeper of our happy memories
And the little black box where my ashes rest.

Chapter 7

That year Ma passed away, peacefully as she always believed it should be. It was the year 2001, I was sixty one and Ma just had turned eighty one. I came to realize that I never had a family of my own. My life had evolved around the devotion for The Duchess and Ma. Now only their memories filled what I felt, an enormous emptiness. Left only with a great desire to develop the thinking my father started, I decided to move on and continue where my golden trail was supposed to take me.

I let myself go and decided to move north. I always wanted to fly North and high. This was the opportunity to do so. I always heard that one could live a peaceful life in Canada and peace is what I needed, most conducive to undisturbed thinking. So there I went.

When moving I discovered that I did not own much. Mostly everything I had, remained in my head, like when I was a little kid. Amazing that you are able to carry a whole life just in the very small confines of our mind!

Once in Toronto, I settled myself around Mount Pleasant and started the necessary paper work to stay for good. The first time I saw Mount Pleasant I thought it was the most beautiful park I had ever seen, I didn't know it was a cemetery.

During one of those conversations that one has with oneself. I though, how convenient, I am starting a new life and at the same time found the most beautiful place I have ever seen, to eventually rest in peace. I smile of my cynicism, but I knew then it was the place I wanted for my final resting place. Right away I started to make plans as to how to end up there.

I made it a habit to take long walks, enjoying the magnificent surroundings and getting familiar with a nice location I'd selected to be my final resting place. It was already early autumn and the colors of the maple trees had turned into an array of yellows, pinks, okras and reds; all of which made me take a blame for not having discovered such wonder, earlier this past summer.

Well it's never too late, I reasoned and prepared to go through the cycle this year and actually walk the grounds, with the purpose of getting more familiar.

And I came across this large mausoleum. It had room for about ten people, of which only five had been used. The family name was Eaton. I recognized them as a very prominent family within the realms of Canadian society, because many things are still named after them, local royalty you may say. The mausoleum was very visible among the other tombs of the cemetery and the name of Timothy Eaton was highlighted, I could tell. To have a plot like this you had to have at least one hundred and fifty years of prominent position and a lot of money, I thought.

Upon all this vision I stumbled over the idea that I could mention this description in my next book and stablish the fact that since there was no way for my ashes to end up legitimately on such a lavish place, I wholeheartedly wished that my ashes would be powdered near the roots of the nearest wiping willow to the mausoleum, inconspicuously without any sign or marking.

Only my account of this wish, printed in the proper place of my next book to testify to the fact, and maybe in addition the account of those who accomplished my very unorthodox final wish, as further proof of it been completed according to my mandate. At the time I completely forgot that often people change their minds, including me.

***

When I reached the peak, standing on the plateau, appeared this enormous stone wall, two stores high and built with large stones, carved probably thousands of years ago. It was old. I was old too. This similitude had a tranquilizing effect then. I looked sideways and could see no end to the wall. I look up and also could see no end.

However, there was a gigantic door. Imposing and carved out of the hearth of an ancient cedar tree. There was no way to make an impression of any kind on that door with my fragile hands. Unexpectedly, slowly it did slide open just enough for me to see what was on the other side. There, in my version, I actually saw a trail curving through the forest and it was golden. The beautiful golden tone that only the Canadian autumn maple leaves give nature to frame ones path.

At that moment, I realized I spent my whole life the way I wished it was and then I found out it wasn't the way I wished it was. It was a signal. Not only meant that I must finish my work, but the title revealed itself, *The Golden Trail*. It became obvious then that my next book should attempt to define the meaning of existence, not less. What are we here for? How should we organize ourselves to efficiently accomplish that purpose?

And establish that religion and government should be based on the respect and conservation of life and promotion of knowledge in all its aspects, never based on ignorance and fear.

The best religion I know is to respect life (past or present) in all its forms. Life is essentially constant and perpetual change, therefore it needs no mayor intervention from us, simply the recognition that everything is alive and that is all we are. In our present conception, as time goes by, God looks more and more like man and the universe looks more and more like God.

***

One night while looking at the stars, I felt someone was also looking at me from a million light years away. What puzzles me the most about life is that it has to end to continue. The universe never had a beginning and will never have an end, simply evolves, so the probability of not being life somewhere else in the universe is simply zero.

We live full aware of our ultimate disillusion, death. Nothing should then matter, but it does. Otherwise life would be a sad long wait. No one is really original, just mere copies of the same old formula. Only some look at these thoughts from a different perspective; sometimes brilliantly.

The most unique aspect about us is me not being you and you not being me. Science is the inspiration of art or….Is it art the inspiration of science? In addition, to assume that the universe is finite is to lower the level of the mighty concept. It was clear that all these concepts had to be put in writing. I knew that as I became older I began to appreciate more life and simple things, and that was to my advantage.

I became involved in nostalgia as I pondered about these views and took a pause to remember a poem I wrote specially for the woman that would eventually have the responsibility to turn my bones into ashes, at whatever time they were not able to sustain a body that refused to be alive, whenever she came along.

***

The following months I reflected a lot about life and came to the conclusion that I have lived a good life and when my time comes up I wish to die in a dream, from which I never wake up. Where I and everyone I love were very happy and surrounded by the most pleasant music. Sometimes, while thinking about dying I imagined that it was like drifting on a raft into the nothingness of a vast sea, knowing that there was no return and nowhere else to go, only emptiness and bottomless ahead.

Then I came across the thought that my life could have been as easy as sailing across a quite lake on a nice summer day, if I had a different legacy. Really, I was forced to survive, I had no other choice.

But how did I survive? Sometimes I didn't, as a matter of speech. I lighted up candles and oil lamps, said prayers and venerated images, hoping they would do it for me. They did but only when I added some action of my own.

I remember my father as a very tall man standing beside me and an even taller silhouette of a shadow projected towards the east. Latter own, in my version, I presumed that he came home from his daily working day. Around three o clock everyday he would pick me up, placing one hand under my right underarm and lifting me like a feather towards him. Holding me close to his chest and saying "How is my Facundo today?" With a gentle voice, hardly believable to come from such corpulent body, so I made believe it was coming from the depth of his soul. That small question filled my existence at the time and it impressed how much he loved me.

My father used to take me with him, on some of his trips. One time he took me to the small little town where he was born. I remember when we were driving on the way, along the Andes, besides the hills, just before we turned a nice curb of the countryside, he said,

> *"Facundo the thing about the mountains is that they inspire you to live. The morning due and fresh air is the gift of nature to show us how happy one can be, if only you let it be. If one could join, the dynamic of the city, with the tranquility of the mountains. If one could only have the best of both worlds, but we can't! So the conclusion is that one should enjoy life, in its own context, in its own time."*

He said, sitting at the wheel of the car, while curving along the slope and marveling with each turn at the beauty of the landscape.

***

The months passed and I continued to reflect more about life. It was so evident that life was but a flicker of the eye. It would have no meaning at all if it wasn't for our imagination, our ability to interpret events and the construction of a certain reality out of perception and ultimately through consciousness.

The significance of events has always astonished me, how we shape and reshape events. Our best quality is the ability to shape and reshape the significance of events and what is more to discard what we find is not relevant to us. What is the significance of life, if not learning as we go and leaving memories as we part? I only had a few friends and when it was time to leave, I would do it without remorse or ill feelings.

Everything is a part of the same thing, interconnected by the never ending cycle of contraction and expansion, which is eternal. Life and death are the same elements in a different state, like water is to ice.

"As you wish, if that makes you happy!"

I said to myself, in a moment of tenderness.

***

During my journey North, I had to relate to many people, some good, some bad, some awful. Curiously I learned a lot from each one of them. All in their own way helped me to continue.

Some were humble, some arrogant, some rich and some poor. From this mix I learned that money and power greatly distorts the reality of our life. This observation, above all helped me understand that we all depend unavoidably on each other.

I learned that humility and compassion makes us strong, arrogance makes us weak and insecure, open mindedness reassures us and humor is the savior.

If I have only one quality to choose it will be humility. Humility is the most powerful of virtues and the most difficult to practice. Make me fail and I will be humble, so I do not make the mistake of becoming arrogant. That will be in itself success.

**

In time I had to decide while writing *The Golden Trail*, whether it would be an autobiography, a memoir, or a novel. In time I realized that it didn't matter, because everything was based on imagination and ultimately everyone acts a plot, with profusion of descriptions, conclusions, scenes and dialogues. So I just told the story and let the reader decide.

By now I have learned not to get attached to material things. I can buy them, sell them, even loose them and it doesn't affect me. I use one of my disbeliefs, "I think I can always get them back again, because I am eternal", to my advantage. It worked.

**

Chapter 8

It took me two years after The Duchess passed away, to find out that I was not completely alone in this world. True, my life had been reduced to almost nothing for many years. Then I realized that I had spent three quarters of my life trying to make The Duchess understand that we belonged together, until she ran out of time…

Truly, now the only valid alternative I had in life was the pursuit of a little well deserved happiness and I knew the key of it all was finding somehow to love. But love comes in many shapes and forms, sometimes hiding in the most inaccessible places and sometimes unexpectedly appearing in the spur of the moment, as an almost imperceptible whiff, which only those marked by destiny are bound to recognize.

Obviously I didn't know how much can life bring along at the right time, if you let it. To me it was the dream of having a home, someone else to strive for and a feeling of "having it" any time, because it was just an arm away from my side of the bed…

And so, eventually it did appear for me in the form of a petite Asian lady. Who caught first my attention, then my interest, subsequently my devotion, ultimately my love and finally became my entire life. In Chinese she was called Pik Yuk. In real life I called her "The Princess".

Our love developed slowly, continuously and naturally, nurtured by actions of respect and a feeling of content with each other. Early on, we did away with the elaborate formalities and the little gimmicks that people use in an effort to make each other appear more attractive.

We felt no need for that, because our souls were communicating freely and unadorned we settled immediately to the business of being useful and supportive to each other, in a simple but almost perfect way. Such a good luck does not come often, and sometimes when it does it is disregarded as unimportant. What a mistake!

We recognized our existence as valuable immediately with grace, and took advantage of every bit of opportunity to begin building our future without delay.

Early on we also accepted luck as an important factor in our lives. Not that we would gamble our lives away, but we noticed that without a little bit of luck nothing happens. Luck is one of the ingredients that make dreams come true.

As a fact, we ourselves were a clear product of luck. So to give this belief a practical use, we have been playing the lottery since we met. I know, you may be thinking that the odds are always so astronomical that it could seem like a waste of time. That is true, but on the other hand someone has to win it. So if you buy one ticket you have one chance, if you don't, you have no chance.

We buy a weekly ticket religiously and we believe that someday we shall win the jackpot. Why not, we have been consistently lucky in so many other aspects of our life that when it happens, it would feel very natural.

***

Our mutual discovery happened sixteen years ago (in 2001) in a little mall in Toronto, where we met for coffee, and which we still visit from time to time, in honor and memory that miracles still happen to those who mean well. I always had the tendency to dramatize and romanticize! Well after all we have to admit that life is full of drama and romance. One can't exist without the other.

Well, sixteen years have passed since 2001 and I am still here, breathing the air that allows me to think and be grateful. I had nothing when I came into her life. I'd given everything away along the way. She had a small apartment and took me in and my suitcase generously, without expecting anything in return.

I have since published *The Golden Trail*, in honor of my father the first Facundo Marval and I have more stories to tell and new expectations for the future.

I am currently writing a collection of poems and a novel in The Princes' honor. Is the least I could do. All as a celebration of life or as some people put it *"To leave a legacy"*, because let's face it good books do not sell well, they just last longer, much longer... They transcend.

Between you and I, it is really an attempt to make memories last a little longer after my departure. It is true, that we ultimately die when the very last person has ceased to recall the very last memory about us. Until then, we float like some kind of energy from mind to mind, and interestingly enough it is the nearest thing to actually being alive. That is why some people never entirely disappear!

My life is substantially better because of The Princess and the fact that I have someone special to love. Though I still have to continue to find meaning in life and strive for happiness, which does not come easy. At times feeling a little lonely perhaps, during those moments of solitude, but I dismiss them as the price to pay for being a little creative, thinking that it will be all worth it at the end.

***

It was our destiny. In search of a little happiness I moved Northbound and "The Princess" Westbound, the traditional ways to look for opportunity. We ended up meeting in Toronto. Once again trying to construct a family, she for the second time and I for the third time.

I concluded that families must be painstakingly built, they do not come ready-made. The ingredients are primarily communication and love, which eventually results in a high level of trust, which in turn allows people to collaborate and flourish in harmony. I deposited all my trust in "The Princess" and began to do things together, towards common security and wellbeing. Respect, communication, finance, dreams, health, a couple forever...

No hope of perfection because there never is. I don't know if men and women realize how fragile they are. Never forget, that the relationship between a man and a woman is based only on very bridle trust.

In addition, women by having the power to certify the human gene do carry an immense responsibility. We owe this miracle to them. Many loves have been broken by frail passing winds, even though made of solid oak, if it wasn't for the perseverance of women to keep families together at all cost. We couldn't even if we tried give them enough recognition.

Because our minds perceive reality in different ways there is not only one reality. There are as many realities as people. It all depends on the way we feel it, perceive it, and express it. Sometimes this is very difficult to understand, especially when points of view are very different, in which case only flexibility and compromise helps.

***

Most of the important things in my life have come unsought. I have learned to recognize what is placed in my path, and accept what I think is meant for me. This is the most natural way for me to make decisions. Although life has shown me that it is not the most convenient way, I would do it again.

I had to dig deep into the fabric of life to find the little moments of happiness that I have. Mostly they happened, when I was able to give, to those near and dear to me, or when I was able to receive affection from those who chose to love me. I have to admit that I also had some joy from trivial things, often after dreaming for years about them, a little watch here, a little car there…but nothing compared to the feeling of wellbeing that providing for the ones you love brings.

I'm so identified with my own life that I do not conceive it otherwise. I see myself as somebody who has only one form and a certain unique identity and I cannot think about it differently. Arguably, "My life has only one life." Perhaps I choose the hardest way. But "Easy comes, easy goes. Hardly comes….hardly goes?"

***

Incidentally, the other day, while sitting on a bench in the park, I asked myself: "Would I be still alive next spring?" and I was not able to answer. I had great doubts. It was not a good feeling even though it was only a premonition. I only wish when my time comes, the great forces of nature allow me to die in peace with myself and others, without leaving behind any suffering to anyone and possibly something useful for some.

Dreaming about something pleasant, like those amazing mango trees of Little Venice - my original country - swaying to the compass of the breeze, cooling off the tropical heat, as giant elephant ears. Always green, always leafy, always shady, always generous and always beautiful. The dear mango trees of my country, the always dear mangos of my youth.

I liked to think life was something like going to school, attended all the courses, learned everything there was to learn, eventually approved all the exams with high marks and graduated with honors!

***

Time has passed relentlessly but not in vain. I have learned a few things, done a few more and most of all lived in my own terms, in peace. I ceased a long time ago to be "somebody" and chose to become "useful", retiring to the arts with passion.

My greatest fortune has been to be a free soul and hang to the belief that the revolution of the mind ultimately wins.

~

The mind is everything

~

ACKNOWLEDGEMENTS

My wife Jacqueline gave me unconditional support. My two daughters Carla and Beatriz nourished my soul with much needed love. Their mother, Beatriz Marquez (May she rest in peace) was my inspiration. John Miller and the Toronto's Writers Cooperative gifted me with invaluable critique. Dr. Bruce M. Sutton continues to take care of my psychological wounds and Dr. Bodhan Olearczyk keeps my body functioning.

Thanks! Without you all, this book never would have been written or published.

The author in 2015

Luis Carlos Márquez lives in Toronto. The author of *This Marquez Thing* (a memoir), *Twelve Farewell Poems* (selected poems), *A Day in The Park* (a short story) and now *The Personal Revolution of Facundo Marval* (a novel). Four genres and one unique voice.

www.ingramcontent.com/pod-product-compliance
Lightning Source LLC
Chambersburg PA
CBHW060210290526
45789CB00003B/1228